SUCCESSFUL COOKING

ONE-POTS

INDEX

Contents

Hot Beef Borscht   4

Lamb Hotpot   6

Pasta and Bean Soup   8

Mulligatawny   10

Beef Pho   12

Avgolemono with Chicken   14

Chunky Vegetable Soup   16

Clam Chowder   18

Chicken, Leek and Sweet Potato One-pot   20

Thai Beef and Pumpkin Curry   22

Green Tofu Curry   24

Pork Vindaloo   26

Coconut Seafood and Tofu Curry   28

Thai Duck and Pineapple Curry   30

Panang Beef   32

Balti Chicken   34

Spiced Beef and Potatoes   36

Pork and Coriander Stew   38

Seafood and Fennel Stew   40

Lentil Bhujia Stew   42

Sukiyaki   44

Ponzu Chicken and Noodle Hotpot   46

Bean and Capsicum Stew   48

Lamb's Liver and Bacon Stew   50

Beef Bourguignonne   52

Creamy Garlic Seafood Stew   54

Greek Octopus Stew   56

Steak and Kidney Stew   58

Pork and Eggplant Hotpot   60

Moroccan Seafood with Coriander   62

Vegetarian Chilli   64

Chilli Con Pollo   66

Spanish Chicken and Rice Stew   68

Ratatouille   70

Stuffed Squid Stew   72

Creamy Veal and Mushroom Stew   74

Lemon and Rosemary Chicken Stew   76

Beef Pot Roast   78

Hot Beef Borscht

PREPARATION TIME: 30 minutes

TOTAL COOKING TIME: 2 hours 50 minutes

SERVES 4–6

500 g (1 lb) gravy beef, cut into large pieces
500 g (1 lb) fresh beetroot
1 onion, finely chopped
1 carrot, cut into short strips
1 parsnip, cut into short strips
1 cup (75 g/2½ oz) finely shredded cabbage
sour cream and chopped fresh chives,
  to serve

1 Put the beef and 1 litre water in a large, heavy-based saucepan, and bring slowly to the boil. Reduce the heat, cover and simmer for 1 hour. Skim the surface as required.

2 Cut the stems from the beetroot, wash well and place in a large, heavy-based saucepan with 1 litre water. Bring to the boil, then reduce the heat and simmer for 40 minutes, or until tender. Drain, reserving 1 cup (250 ml/8 fl oz) of the liquid. Cool, then peel and grate the beetroot.

3 Remove the meat from the stock, cool and dice. Skim any fat from the surface of the stock. Return the meat to the stock and add the onion, carrot, parsnip, beetroot and reserved liquid. Bring to the boil, reduce the heat, cover and simmer for 45 minutes.

4 Stir in the cabbage and simmer for a further 15 minutes. Season to taste. Serve with the sour cream and chives.

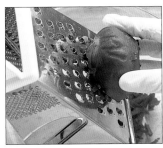

To avoid stains, wear rubber gloves to grate the cooled beetroot.

Allow the meat to cool, then cut it into dice using a sharp knife.

Pour the reserved beetroot liquid into the soup and bring to the boil.

Lamb Hotpot

PREPARATION TIME: 40 minutes + 1 hour
refrigeration
TOTAL COOKING TIME: 2 hours
SERVES 4

2 tablespoons olive oil
8 lamb shanks
2 onions, sliced
4 cloves garlic, finely chopped
3 bay leaves, torn in half
1–2 teaspoons hot paprika
2 teaspoons sweet paprika
1 tablespoon plain flour
1/4 cup (60 g/2 oz) tomato paste
1.5 litres vegetable stock
4 potatoes, chopped
4 carrots, sliced
3 celery sticks, thickly sliced
3 tomatoes, seeded and chopped

1 To make the lamb stock, heat 1 tablespoon of the oil in a large, heavy-based saucepan over medium heat. Brown the shanks well in two batches, then drain on paper towels.

2 Add the remaining oil to the pan and cook the onion, garlic and bay leaves over low heat for 10 minutes, stirring regularly. Add the paprikas and flour and cook, stirring, for 2 minutes. Gradually add the combined tomato paste and vegetable stock. Bring to the boil, stirring continuously, and return the shanks to the pan. Reduce the heat to low and simmer, covered, for 1½ hours, stirring occasionally.

3 Remove and discard the bay leaves. Remove the shanks, allow to cool slightly and then cut the meat from the bone. Discard the bone. Cut the meat into pieces and refrigerate. Refrigerate the stock for about 1 hour, or until fat forms on the surface and can be spooned off.

4 Return the meat to the stock along with the potato, carrot and celery, and bring to the boil. Reduce the heat and simmer for 15 minutes. Season, and add the chopped tomato to serve.

Halve the tomatoes and scoop out the seeds with a teaspoon.

Stir the paprikas and flour into the onion mixture until it just begins to colour.

Spoon off the fat that forms on the surface of the soup.

Pasta and Bean Soup

PREPARATION TIME: 15 minutes +
overnight soaking + 10 minutes resting
TOTAL COOKING TIME: 1 hour 45 minutes
SERVES 4

200 g (6½ oz) dried borlotti beans
¼ cup (60 ml/2 fl oz) olive oil
90 g (3 oz) piece pancetta, finely diced
1 onion, finely chopped
2 cloves garlic, crushed
1 celery stick, thinly sliced
1 carrot, diced
1 bay leaf
1 sprig fresh rosemary
1 sprig fresh flat-leaf parsley
400 g (13 oz) can diced tomatoes, drained
1.6 litres vegetable stock
2 tablespoons finely chopped fresh flat-leaf
  parsley
150 g (5 oz) ditalini or other small
  dried pasta
extra virgin olive oil, to serve
grated fresh Parmesan, to serve

1 Place the beans in a large bowl, cover with cold water and leave to soak overnight. Drain and rinse.

2 Heat the oil in a large saucepan, add the pancetta, onion, garlic, celery and carrot, and cook over medium heat for 5 minutes, or until golden. Season with pepper. Add the bay leaf, rosemary, parsley, tomato, stock and beans, and bring to the boil. Reduce the heat and simmer for 1½ hours, or until the beans are tender. Add more boiling water if necessary to maintain the liquid level.

3 Discard the bay leaf, rosemary and parsley sprigs. Scoop out 1 cup (250 ml/8 fl oz) of the bean mixture and purée in a food processor or blender. Return to the pan, season with salt and ground black pepper, and add the parsley and pasta. Simmer for 6 minutes, or until the pasta is al dente. Remove from the heat and set aside for 10 minutes. Serve drizzled with extra virgin olive oil and sprinkled with Parmesan.

Note: If you prefer, you can use three 400 g (13 oz) cans drained borlotti beans. Simmer with the other vegetables for 30 minutes.

Cook the pancetta, onion, garlic, celery and carrot for 5 minutes.

Purée 1 cup (250 ml/8 fl oz) of the bean mixture in a food processor.

Add the pasta to the soup and simmer until it is al dente.

9

Mulligatawny

PREPARATION TIME: 20 minutes
TOTAL COOKING TIME: 1 hour 15 minutes
SERVES 4

30 g (1 oz) butter
375 g (12 oz) chicken thigh cutlets, skin and
  fat removed
1 large onion, finely chopped
1 apple, peeled, cored and diced
1 tablespoon curry paste
2 tablespoons plain flour
3 cups (750 ml/24 fl oz) chicken stock
1/4 cup (50 g/13/4 oz) basmati rice
1 tablespoon chutney
1 tablespoon lemon juice
1/4 cup (60 ml/2 fl oz) cream

1 Heat the butter in a large heavy-based saucepan. Cook the chicken for 5 minutes, or until browned, then remove and set aside. Add the onion, apple and curry paste to the pan. Cook for 5 minutes, or until the onion is soft. Stir in the flour and cook for 2 minutes, then add half the stock. Stir until the mixture boils and thickens.
2 Return the chicken to the pan with the remaining stock. Stir until boiling, then reduce the heat, cover and simmer for 1 hour. Add the rice for the last 15 minutes of cooking.
3 Remove the chicken from the pan. Remove the meat from the bones, dice finely and return to the pan. Add the chutney, lemon juice and cream, and season to taste.

Once the mixture has thickened, return the browned chicken thighs to the pan.

Add the basmati rice to the soup during the last 15 minutes of cooking.

Add the chutney, lemon juice and cream at the end of cooking.

11

Beef Pho

PREPARATION TIME: 15 minutes +
40 minutes freezing
TOTAL COOKING TIME: 30 minutes
SERVES 4

400 g (13 oz) rump steak, trimmed
1 litre beef stock
1/2 onion
1 star anise
1 cinnamon stick
1 tablespoon fish sauce
pinch ground white pepper
200 g (6 1/2 oz) fresh thin round rice noodles
2 spring onions, thinly sliced
30 fresh Vietnamese mint leaves
1 cup (90 g/3 oz) bean sprouts
1 small white onion, thinly sliced
1 small fresh red chilli, thinly sliced

1 Wrap the meat in plastic wrap and freeze for 30–40 minutes, or until partially frozen. Thinly slice the meat across the grain.

2 Place the stock in a large heavy-based saucepan with the onion half, star anise, cinnamon stick, fish sauce, white pepper and 2 cups (500 ml/16 fl oz) water, and bring to the boil over high heat. Reduce the heat to medium–low and simmer, covered, for 20 minutes. Discard the onion, star anise and cinnamon stick.

3 Meanwhile, cover the noodles with boiling water and gently separate. Drain and refresh with cold water. Divide the noodles and spring onion among the serving bowls. Top with equal amounts of beef, mint, bean sprouts, onion slices and chilli. Ladle the simmering broth into the bowls, and serve.

Note: It is important that the broth is kept hot as the heat will cook the slices of beef.

Thinly slice the partially frozen steak across the grain.

Avgolemono with Chicken

PREPARATION TIME: 30 minutes
TOTAL COOKING TIME: 30 minutes
SERVES 4

1 onion, halved
2 cloves
1 carrot, cut into chunks
1 bay leaf
500 g (1 lb) chicken breast fillets
1/3 cup (75 g/2 1/2 oz) short-grain rice
3 eggs, separated
1/4 cup (60 ml/2 fl oz) lemon juice
2 tablespoons chopped fresh flat-leaf
  parsley
4 thin lemon slices, to garnish

1 Stud the onion halves with the cloves and place in a large saucepan with 1.5 litres water. Add the carrot, bay leaf and chicken. Season with salt and freshly ground black pepper. Slowly bring to the boil, then reduce the heat and simmer for 10 minutes, or until the chicken is cooked.

2 Strain the stock into a clean saucepan, reserving the chicken and discarding the vegetables. Add the rice to the stock, bring to the boil, then reduce the heat and simmer for 15 minutes, or until tender. Tear the chicken into shreds.

3 Whisk the egg whites until stiff peaks form, then beat in the yolks. Slowly beat in the lemon juice. Gently stir in 150 ml (5 fl oz) of the hot (not boiling) soup and beat thoroughly. Add the egg mixture to the soup and stir gently over low heat until thickened slightly. It should still be quite thin. Do not let it boil or the eggs may scramble. Add the shredded chicken, and season.

4 Set aside for 3–4 minutes to allow the flavours to develop, then sprinkle with the parsley. Garnish with the lemon slices and serve immediately.

Simmer the chicken breast fillets for 10 minutes, or until cooked.

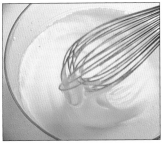

Gently stir some of the hot soup into the egg mixture and beat thoroughly.

Add the shredded chicken breast fillets to the soup.

Chunky Vegetable Soup

PREPARATION TIME: 20 minutes +
overnight soaking
TOTAL COOKING TIME: 1 hour 5 minutes
SERVES 6

1/2 cup (100 g/3 1/2 oz) dried red kidney
  beans or borlotti beans
1 tablespoon olive oil
1 leek, halved lengthways, chopped
1 small onion, diced
2 carrots, chopped
2 celery sticks, chopped
1 large zucchini, chopped
1 tablespoon tomato paste
1 litre vegetable stock
400 g (13 oz) pumpkin, cut into 2 cm (3/4
  inch) cubes
2 potatoes, cut into 2 cm (3/4 inch) cubes
1/4 cup (7 g/1/4 oz) chopped fresh flat-leaf
  parsley

1 Put the beans in a large bowl, cover with cold water and soak overnight. Rinse, then transfer to a saucepan, cover with cold water and cook for 45 minutes, or until just tender. Drain.

2 Meanwhile, heat the oil in a large saucepan. Add the leek and onion, and cook over medium heat for 2–3 minutes without browning, or until they start to soften. Add the carrot, celery and zucchini, and cook for 3–4 minutes. Add the tomato paste and stir for a further 1 minute. Pour in the stock and 1.25 litres water, and bring to the boil. Reduce the heat to low and simmer for 20 minutes.

3 Add the pumpkin, potato, parsley and red kidney beans, and simmer for a further 20 minutes, or until the vegetables are tender and the beans are cooked. Season to taste. Serve immediately with crusty wholemeal or wholegrain bread.

Note: To save time, use a 420 g (14 oz) can of red kidney beans instead of dried beans.

Using a sharp knife, cut the
peeled pumpkin into large
cubes.

Add the vegetables and beans,
and simmer until the vegetables
are cooked.

Clam Chowder

PREPARATION TIME: 25 minutes

TOTAL COOKING TIME: 45 minutes

SERVES 4

30 g (1 oz) butter
2 rashers bacon, finely chopped
1 large onion, finely chopped
4 potatoes, cut into small cubes
2 cups (500 ml/16 fl oz) fish stock
1 bay leaf
1/2 cup (125 ml/4 fl oz) milk
4 x 105 g (3 1/2 oz) cans baby clams, drained
  and chopped
1/4 cup (15 g/1/2 oz) finely chopped fresh
  parsley
1 cup (250 ml/8 fl oz) cream

1 Heat the butter in a large saucepan. Cook the bacon and onion for 2–3 minutes, or until softened. Stir in the potato. Cook for a further 2–3 minutes, then gradually pour on the stock. Add the bay leaf.

2 Bring the mixture to the boil, then reduce the heat and simmer, covered, for 20 minutes, or until the potato is cooked. Simmer for 10 minutes, or until the soup is reduced and slightly thickened. Discard the bay leaf.

3 Add the milk, chopped clams, parsley and cream. Stir to reheat, but do not allow the soup to boil. Season with salt and freshly ground black pepper.

Peel and cut the potatoes into strips and then into small cubes.

Remove the bay leaf from the chowder with a pair of tongs.

Add the milk, chopped clams and parsley, and pour in the cream.

19

Chicken, Leek and Sweet Potato One-pot

PREPARATION TIME: 15 minutes

TOTAL COOKING TIME: 1 hour 40 minutes

SERVES 4

600 g (1¼ lb) orange sweet potato
2 tablespoons olive oil
1.5 kg (3 lb) chicken pieces
1 leek, cut into 2 cm (¾ inch) slices
2 cloves garlic, crushed
2 tablespoons plain flour
2 cups (500 ml/16 fl oz) chicken stock
2 tablespoons fresh thyme

1 Preheat the oven to hot 220°C (425°F/Gas 7). Peel the sweet potato and cut it into chunks. Heat 1 tablespoon of the oil in a large flameproof casserole dish. Cook the chicken in batches for 3–4 minutes, or until browned. Set aside. Add the remaining oil and cook the leek and garlic for 2 minutes, or until soft.

2 Add the flour to the dish and cook, stirring, for about 1 minute to brown the flour. Gradually add the stock, stirring until the sauce boils and thickens. Remove from the heat. Return the chicken to the pan.

3 Add the sweet potato and half the thyme. Bake, covered, for 1½ hours, or until the chicken is cooked through and the sweet potato is tender. Season, and scatter with the remaining thyme. Serve with steamed rice.

Brown the chicken pieces, in batches, until they are browned all over.

Gradually add the stock to the flour mixture, then stir until the sauce boils and thickens.

Add the sweet potato pieces to the casserole dish, along with half the thyme.

Thai Beef and Pumpkin Curry

PREPARATION TIME: 20 minutes
TOTAL COOKING TIME: 1 hour 30 minutes
SERVES 6

2 tablespoons oil
750 g (1½ lb) blade steak, thinly sliced
4 tablespoons curry paste (or according
   to taste)
2 cloves garlic, finely chopped
1 onion, sliced lengthways
6 curry leaves, torn
3 cups (750 ml/24 fl oz) coconut milk
450 g (14 oz) butternut pumpkin, roughly
   diced
2 tablespoons chopped unsalted peanuts
1 tablespoon palm sugar or soft brown
   sugar
2 tablespoons tamarind purée
2 tablespoons fish sauce
curry leaves, extra, to garnish

1 Heat a wok or frying pan over high heat. Add the oil and swirl to coat the side. Add the meat in batches and cook for 5 minutes, or until browned. Remove the meat from the wok.

2 Add the curry paste, garlic, onion and curry leaves to the wok, and stir to coat. Return the meat to the wok and cook, stirring, over medium heat for 2 minutes.

3 Add the coconut milk to the wok, then reduce the heat and simmer for 45 minutes. Add the diced pumpkin and simmer for 25–30 minutes, or until the meat and the vegetables are tender and the sauce has thickened.

4 Stir in the peanuts, palm sugar, tamarind purée and fish sauce, and simmer for 1 minute. Garnish with curry leaves. Serve with steamed rice.

Cut the meat across the grain and at an angle into thin slices.

Add the meat to the wok and cook in batches until browned.

Simmer until the meat and vegetables are tender and the sauce has thickened.

23

Green Tofu Curry

PREPARATION TIME: 20 minutes
TOTAL COOKING TIME: 20 minutes
SERVES 6

Curry Paste
10 small fresh green chillies
50 g (1¾ oz) red Asian shallots, peeled
2 cloves garlic
1 cup (50 g/1¾ oz) finely chopped coriander
  stems and roots
1 stem lemon grass (white part only), chopped
2 tablespoons grated fresh galangal
1 tablespoon ground coriander
1 teaspoon ground cumin
1 teaspoon black peppercorns
½ teaspoon ground turmeric
1 tablespoon lime juice

2 tablespoons oil
1 onion, sliced
400 ml (13 fl oz) can coconut cream
4–5 kaffir lime leaves, torn
500 g (1 lb) firm tofu, cut into 2 cm (¾ inch) cubes
1 tablespoon lime juice
1 tablespoon shredded fresh Thai basil

1 To make the curry paste, place all the ingredients in a food processor and process until smooth.
2 Heat the oil in a frying pan, add the onion and cook for 5 minutes, or until soft. Add 4 tablespoons curry paste (or more for a stronger flavour) and cook, stirring, for 2 minutes. Stir in the coconut cream and 1 cup (250 ml/8 fl oz) water, and season with salt. Bring to the boil and add the lime leaves and tofu. Reduce the heat and simmer for 8 minutes, stirring often. Stir in the lime juice and Thai basil, and serve.

Note: The recipe for the curry paste makes 1 cup, but you will only need ⅓ cup. Freeze the remaining paste in two portions to use at a later date.

Place the curry paste ingredients in a food processor and process until smooth.

Cook the onion slices for 5 minutes, or until the onion is soft.

Pork Vindaloo

PREPARATION TIME: 20 minutes
TOTAL COOKING TIME: 2 hours
SERVES 4

1/4 cup (60 ml/2 fl oz) oil
1 kg (2 lb) pork fillets, cut into bite-size
  pieces
2 onions, finely chopped
4 cloves garlic, finely chopped
1 tablespoon finely chopped fresh ginger
1 tablespoon garam masala
2 teaspoons brown mustard seeds
4 tablespoons vindaloo paste

1 Heat the oil in a saucepan, add the pork in small batches and cook over medium heat for 5–7 minutes, or until browned. Remove from the pan.

2 Add the onion, garlic, ginger, garam masala and mustard seeds to the pan, and cook, stirring, for 5 minutes, or until the onion is soft.

3 Return all the meat to the pan, add the vindaloo paste and cook, stirring, for 2 minutes. Add 2½ cups (625 ml/l21 fl oz) water and bring to the boil. Reduce the heat and simmer, covered, for 1½ hours, or until the meat is tender. Serve with boiled rice and pappadums.

Trim the pork of any excess fat or sinew and cut into cubes.

Cook the pork in small batches over medium heat until browned.

Add the vindaloo paste to the pan, and cook until the meat is tender.

Coconut Seafood and Tofu Curry

PREPARATION TIME: 30 minutes

TOTAL COOKING TIME: 30 minutes

SERVES 4

2 tablespoons soy bean oil, or oil

500 g (1 lb) firm white fish (ling, perch), cut into 2 cm (3/4 inch) cubes

250 g (8 oz) raw prawns, peeled and deveined, tails intact

2 x 400 ml (13 fl oz) cans coconut milk

1 tablespoon red curry paste

4 fresh or 8 dried kaffir lime leaves

2 tablespoons fish sauce

2 tablespoons finely chopped fresh lemon grass (white part only)

2 cloves garlic, crushed

1 tablespoon finely chopped fresh galangal

1 tablespoon shaved palm sugar or soft brown sugar

300 g (10 oz) silken firm tofu, cut into 1.5 cm (5/8 inch) cubes

1/2 cup (125 g/4 oz) bamboo shoots, julienned

1 large fresh red chilli, thinly sliced

2 teaspoons lime juice

spring onions, chopped, to garnish

fresh coriander leaves, chopped, to garnish

1 Heat the oil in a large frying pan or wok over medium heat. Sear the fish and prawns for 1 minute on each side. Remove the fish and prawns from the pan.

2 Place 1/4 cup (60 ml/2 fl oz) of the coconut milk and the curry paste in the pan, and cook over medium heat for 2 minutes, or until fragrant and the oil separates. Add the remaining coconut milk, kaffir lime leaves, fish sauce, lemon grass, garlic, galangal, palm sugar and 1 teaspoon salt. Cook over low heat for 15 minutes.

3 Add the tofu cubes, bamboo shoots and sliced chilli. Simmer for a further 3–5 minutes. Return to medium heat, add the seafood and lime juice, and cook for a further 3 minutes, or until the seafood is just cooked. Remove from the heat.

4 Serve the curry with steamed rice and garnish with the spring onion and coriander leaves.

Peel the prawns, remove the veins and keep the tails intact.

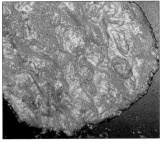

Cook the coconut milk and the curry paste until the oil separates.

Add the tofu, bamboo shoots and chilli, then simmer for 5 minutes.

Thai Duck and Pineapple Curry

PREPARATION TIME: 10 minutes

TOTAL COOKING TIME: 15 minutes

SERVES 4–6

1 tablespoon peanut oil

8 spring onions, sliced on the diagonal into 3 cm (1¼ inch) lengths

2 cloves garlic, crushed

2–4 tablespoons red curry paste

750 g (1¼ lb) Chinese roast duck, chopped

400 ml (13 fl oz) can coconut milk

450 g (14 oz) can pineapple pieces in syrup, drained

3 kaffir lime leaves

¼ cup (15 g/½ oz) chopped fresh coriander

2 tablespoons chopped fresh mint

1 Heat a wok until very hot, add the peanut oil and swirl to coat the side. Add the spring onion, garlic and red curry paste, and stir-fry for 1 minute, or until fragrant.

2 Add the roast duck pieces, coconut milk, drained pineapple pieces, kaffir lime leaves, and half the fresh coriander and mint. Bring to the boil, then reduce the heat and simmer for 10 minutes, or until the duck is heated through and the sauce has thickened slightly. Stir in the remaining fresh coriander and mint, and serve with steamed jasmine rice.

Heat a wok until very hot, add the peanut oil and swirl to coat.

Stir-fry the spring onion, garlic and red curry paste until fragrant.

Simmer until the duck is heated through and the sauce has thickened slightly.

31

Panang Beef

PREPARATION TIME: 30 minutes +
5 minutes soaking
TOTAL COOKING TIME: 1 hour 30 minutes
SERVES 4–6

Curry Paste
8–10 large dried red chillies
6 red Asian shallots, chopped
6 cloves garlic, chopped
1 teaspoon ground coriander
1 tablespoon ground cumin
1 teaspoon white pepper
2 stems lemon grass (white part only),
   bruised and sliced
1 tablespoon chopped fresh galangal
6 coriander roots
2 teaspoons shrimp paste
2 tablespoons roasted peanuts
peanut oil, if needed

1 tablespoon peanut oil
400 ml (13 fl oz) can coconut cream
   (do not shake the can)
1 kg (2 lb) round or blade steak,
   thinly sliced
400 ml (13 fl oz) can coconut milk
4 kaffir lime leaves, whole
1/3 cup (90 g/3 oz) crunchy peanut
   butter
1/4 cup (60 ml/2 fl oz) lime juice
2 1/2 tablespoons fish sauce
3–4 tablespoons palm sugar or soft
   brown sugar
fresh Thai basil leaves, to garnish
1 tablespoon chopped peanuts,
   extra, to garnish (optional)

1 To make the curry paste, soak the chillies in boiling water for 5 minutes, or until soft. Remove the stem and seeds, then chop. Place all the curry paste ingredients in a food processor and process to a smooth paste. Add a little peanut oil if it is too thick.

2 Place the oil and the thick cream from the top of the coconut cream (reserving the rest) in a large saucepan over high heat. Add 6–8 tablespoons of the curry paste and cook, stirring, for 5 minutes, or until fragrant. Cook for 5–10 minutes, or until the coconut cream splits and becomes oily.

3 Add the beef, the reserved coconut cream, coconut milk, lime leaves and peanut butter, and cook for 8 minutes, or until the beef just starts to change colour. Reduce the heat and simmer for 1 hour, or until the beef is tender.

4 Stir in the lime juice, fish sauce and palm sugar, and transfer to a serving dish. Garnish with the Thai basil leaves, and extra peanuts, if desired, and serve immediately.

Place all the curry paste ingredients in a food processor and process until smooth.

Cook the coconut cream and curry paste until it splits and becomes oily.

33

Balti Chicken

PREPARATION TIME: 25 minutes
TOTAL COOKING TIME: 1 hour
SERVES 6

1 kg (2 lb) chicken thigh fillets
1/3 cup (80 ml/2³/4 fl oz) oil
1 large red onion, finely chopped
4–5 cloves garlic, finely chopped
1 tablespoon grated fresh ginger
2 teaspoons ground cumin
2 teaspoons ground coriander
1 teaspoon ground turmeric
1/2 teaspoon chilli powder
425 g (14 oz) can chopped tomatoes
1 green capsicum, cut into 3 cm (1¹/4 inch)
   cubes
1–2 small fresh green chillies, seeded and
   finely chopped
1/3 cup (20 g/³/4 oz) chopped fresh coriander
2 chopped spring onions, to garnish

1 Remove any excess fat or sinew
from the chicken thigh fillets and
cut into 4–5 pieces.

2 Heat a large wok over high heat, add the oil and
swirl to coat the side. Add the onion and stir-fry
over medium heat for 5 minutes, or until softened
but not browned. Add the garlic and ginger, and
stir-fry for 3 minutes.

3 Add the spices, 1 teaspoon salt and ¼ cup (60
ml/2 fl oz) water. Increase the heat to high and
stir-fry for 2 minutes, or until the mixture has
thickened. Take care not to burn.

4 Add the tomato and 1 cup (250 ml/8 fl oz) water
and cook, stirring often, for a further 10 minutes,
or until the mixture is thick and pulpy and the oil
comes to the surface.

5 Add the chicken to the wok, reduce the heat and
simmer, stirring often, for 15 minutes. Add the
capsicum and chilli, and simmer for 25 minutes, or
until the chicken is tender. Add a little water if the
mixture is too thick. Stir in the coriander and
garnish with the spring onion. Serve with rice.

Note: This curry is traditionally cooked in a Karahi
or Balti pan, which is a round-bottomed, cast-iron,
two-handled dish. A wok makes a good
substitute.

*Remove any excess fat or sinew
from the chicken, then cut it
into even-size pieces.*

*Add the spices, salt and water to
the wok, and cook until
thickened.*

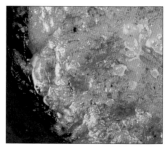

*Cook, stirring, until the mixture
thickens and the oil comes to
the surface.*

Spiced Beef and Potatoes

PREPARATION TIME: 15 minutes
TOTAL COOKING TIME: 1 hour 40 minutes
SERVES 4

Spice Paste
2 onions, chopped
2 cloves garlic, chopped
2 teaspoons grated lemon rind
2 small fresh red chillies, chopped
2 teaspoons ground coriander
2 teaspoons ground cumin
1 teaspoon ground turmeric
1/2 teaspoon ground cardamom
1 teaspoon garam masala

2 tablespoons oil
1 kg (2 lb) lean chuck steak, cut into 3 cm
  (1 1/4 inch) cubes
3/4 cup (185 ml/6 fl oz) coconut cream
1 tablespoon tamarind sauce
500 g (1 lb) baby potatoes, halved

1 To make the spice paste, combine all the ingredients in a food processor or blender, and process for 1 minute, or until very finely chopped.

2 Heat the oil in a heavy-based saucepan. Cook the meat quickly in small batches over medium–high heat until well browned. Drain on paper towels.

3 Add the spice paste to the pan and stir over medium heat for 2 minutes. Return the meat to the pan with the coconut cream, tamarind sauce and 1/2 cup (125 ml/4 fl oz) water, and bring to the boil. Reduce the heat to a simmer and cook, covered, for 30 minutes, stirring occasionally.

4 Add the potato and cook, covered, for 30 minutes. Remove the lid and cook for 30 minutes, or until the meat is tender and almost all of the liquid has evaporated.

Trim the meat of excess fat and sinew and cut it into large cubes.

Return the meat to the pan with the coconut cream, tamarind sauce and water.

Pork and Coriander Stew

PREPARATION TIME: 15 minutes +
overnight marinating
TOTAL COOKING TIME: 1 hour 20 minutes
SERVES 4–6

1½ tablespoons coriander seeds
800 g (1 lb 10 oz) pork fillet, cut into 2 cm
  (¾ inch) cubes
1 tablespoon plain flour
¼ cup (60 ml/2 fl oz) olive oil
1 large onion, thinly sliced
1½ cups (375 ml/12 fl oz) red wine
1 cup (250 ml/8 fl oz) chicken stock
1 teaspoon sugar
sprigs fresh coriander, to garnish

1 Crush the coriander seeds in a mortar and pestle. Combine the pork, crushed seeds and ½ teaspoon cracked pepper in a bowl. Cover and marinate overnight in the refrigerator.

2 Combine the flour and pork, and toss to coat. Heat 2 tablespoons of the oil in a saucepan and cook the pork in batches over high heat for 1–2 minutes, or until brown. Remove.

3 Heat the remaining oil, add the onion and cook over medium heat for 2–3 minutes, or until just golden. Return the meat to the pan, add the red wine, stock and sugar, and season. Bring to the boil, then reduce the heat and simmer, covered, for 1 hour.

4 Remove the meat. Return the pan to the heat and boil over high heat for 3–5 minutes, or until the liquid is reduced and slightly thickened. Pour over the meat and top with coriander.

Heat some oil in a saucepan and cook the pork in batches until brown.

Remove the cooked meat from the pan and keep it warm.

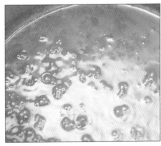

Boil the cooking liquid until it has reduced and slightly thickened.

Seafood and Fennel Stew

PREPARATION TIME: 10 minutes
TOTAL COOKING TIME: 30 minutes
SERVES 6

2 tablespoons olive oil
1 large fennel bulb, thinly sliced
2 leeks, thinly sliced
2 cloves garlic, crushed
1/2 teaspoon paprika
2 tablespoons Pernod or Ricard
200 ml (61/2 fl oz) dry white wine
18 mussels, scrubbed and beards removed
1/4 teaspoon saffron threads
1/4 teaspoon thyme leaves
6 baby octopus
16 raw prawns, peeled and deveined
500 g (1 lb) swordfish steaks, cut into large chunks
400 g (13 oz) baby new potatoes
fennel greens, to garnish

1 Heat the oil in a large saucepan over medium heat. Add the fennel, leek and garlic. Stir in the paprika, season lightly and cook for 8 minutes, or until softened. Add the Pernod and wine, and stir for 1 minute, or until reduced by a third.

2 Add the mussels, discarding any open ones. Cover and cook for 1 minute, or until opened, discarding any that do not open. Remove from the pan to cool; remove from the shells and set aside.

3 Add the saffron and thyme to the pan, and cook for 1–2 minutes, stirring. Adjust the seasoning and transfer to a large, flameproof casserole dish.

4 Use a small sharp knife to remove the octopus heads. Grasp the bodies and push the beaks out with your index finger; remove and discard. Slit the heads and remove the gut. Mix the octopus, prawns, fish and potatoes into the stew. Cover and cook gently for 10 minutes, or until tender. Add the mussels, cover and heat through. Garnish with fennel greens and serve.

Add the Pernod and wine to the softened fennel, leek and garlic mixture.

When the mussels are cool, remove them from their shells.

Cut off the octopus heads. Grasp the body firmly and push out the beak.

41

Lentil Bhujia Stew

PREPARATION TIME: 30 minutes +
overnight soaking + 30 minutes refrigeration
TOTAL COOKING TIME: 1 hour 10 minutes
SERVES 4–6

2 cups (370 g/12 oz) green or brown lentils
1 large onion, grated
1 large potato, grated
1 teaspoon ground cumin
1 teaspoon ground coriander
1 teaspoon ground turmeric
3/4 cup (90 g/3 oz) plain flour
oil, for shallow-frying
2 cloves garlic, crushed
1 tablespoon grated fresh ginger
1 cup (250 ml/8 fl oz) tomato purée
2 cups (500 ml/16 fl oz) vegetable stock
1 cup (250 ml/8 fl oz) cream
200 g (6½ oz) green beans, topped, tailed
  and cut in half
2 carrots, sliced
2 hard-boiled eggs, chopped
sprigs fresh rosemary, to garnish

1 Soak the lentils overnight in cold water. Drain well. Squeeze the excess moisture from the lentils, onion and potato using a tea towel. Place them in a bowl with the ground spices and flour; mix well and leave for 10 minutes. With floured hands, shape the mixture into walnut-sized balls and place on a foil-lined tray. Cover and refrigerate for 30 minutes.

2 Heat 2 cm (¾ inch) of oil in a heavy-based frying pan. Cook the balls in batches over high heat until golden brown. Drain on paper towels.

3 Heat 2 tablespoons of oil in a saucepan and gently fry the garlic and ginger for 2 minutes. Stir in the purée, stock and cream. Bring to the boil, then reduce the heat and simmer for 10 minutes. Add the beans, lentil balls and carrot. Cook, covered, for 30 minutes, stirring twice. Add the egg and cook for 10 minutes. Garnish with rosemary to serve.

VARIATION: Split peas can be used in this recipe in place of the lentils. Soak them in cold water overnight, then drain well before using.

Shape the lentil mixture into walnut-sized balls, and place on a foil-lined tray.

Fry the lentil balls in oil in batches over high heat, until golden brown.

Add the beans, lentil balls and carrot to the simmering sauce.

Sukiyaki

PREPARATION TIME: 10 minutes
TOTAL COOKING TIME: 10 minutes
SERVES 4

Sauce
1/2–1 teaspoon dashi granules
1/3 cup (80 ml/2¾ fl oz) soy sauce
2 tablespoons sake
2 tablespoons mirin
1 tablespoon caster sugar

300 g (10 oz) shirataki noodles (see Note)
50 g (1¾ oz) lard
5 large spring onions, cut into 1 cm (1/2 inch)
  slices on the diagonal
16 fresh shiitake mushrooms, cut into
  smaller pieces if large
800 g (1 lb 10 oz) rump steak, thinly sliced
  across the grain
100 g (3½ oz) watercress, trimmed
4 eggs (optional)

1 To make the sauce, dissolve the dashi granules in 1/2 cup (125 ml/4 fl oz) water. Add the soy sauce, sake, mirin and sugar, and stir until combined.

2 Drain the noodles, then soak them in boiling water for 2 minutes. Rinse in cold water and drain well.

3 Melt the lard in a large frying pan over medium heat. Cook the spring onion, mushrooms and beef in batches, stirring, for 1–2 minutes each batch, or until just brown. Return the meat, spring onion and mushrooms to the pan, then add the sauce and watercress. Cook for 1 minute, or until heated through and the watercress has wilted—the sauce needs to just cover the ingredients but not drown them.

4 To serve, divide the noodles among four serving bowls and spoon the sauce evenly over the top. If desired, crack an egg into each bowl and break up through the sauce using chopsticks until it partially cooks.

Note: Shirataki noodles are sold in Japanese supermarkets.

Rinse the noodles well in a colander, under cold running water.

Add the sauce and watercress, and cook briefly until the watercress has just wilted.

Ponzu Chicken and Noodle Hotpot

PREPARATION TIME: 15 minutes +
overnight refrigeration
TOTAL COOKING TIME: 45 minutes
SERVES 4

Ponzu Sauce
1 tablespoon lemon juice
1 tablespoon lime juice
1 tablespoon rice vinegar
1 tablespoon tamari
1$\frac{1}{2}$ tablespoons mirin
2$\frac{1}{2}$ tablespoons Japanese soy sauce
5 cm (2 inch) piece kombu (kelp), wiped
   with a damp cloth
1 tablespoon bonito flakes

900 g (1 lb 13 oz) chicken thigh cutlets, cut
   in half across the bone
10 cm (4 inch) piece kombu (kelp)
200 g (6$\frac{1}{2}$ oz) dried somen noodles
250 g (8 oz) fresh shiitake mushrooms,
   halved if large
1 carrot, thinly sliced
300 g (10 oz) baby English spinach leaves

1 To make the ponzu sauce, combine all the ingredients in a non-metallic bowl. Cover with plastic wrap and refrigerate overnight, then strain through a fine sieve.
2 Place the chicken and kombu in a large saucepan with 3$\frac{1}{2}$ cups (875 ml/28 fl oz) water. Bring to a simmer over medium heat. Cook for 20 minutes, or until the chicken is cooked, skimming the scum off the surface. Remove the chicken pieces and strain the broth. Transfer the broth and chicken pieces to a 2.5 litre flameproof casserole dish or Japanese nabe. Cover and continue to cook over low heat for 15 minutes.
3 Meanwhile, cook the noodles in a large saucepan of boiling water for 2 minutes, or until tender. Drain and rinse under cold running water.
4 Add the mushrooms and carrot to the chicken, and cook for 5 minutes. Place the noodles on top of the chicken, then top with the spinach. Cook, covered, for 2 minutes, or until the spinach has just wilted. Stir in 4–6 tablespoons of the ponzu sauce, or to taste. Serve immediately.

Cut chicken pieces with a sharp knife.

Bean and Capsicum Stew

PREPARATION TIME: 20 minutes + soaking
TOTAL COOKING TIME: 1 hour 35 minutes
SERVES 4–6

1 cup (200 g/6½ oz) dried haricot beans (see
  Note)
2 tablespoons olive oil
2 large cloves garlic, crushed
1 red onion, halved and cut into thin
  wedges
1 red capsicum, cut into 1.5 cm (⅝ inch)
  squares
1 green capsicum, cut into 1.5 cm (⅝ inch)
  squares
2 x 400 g (13 oz) cans chopped tomatoes
2 tablespoons tomato paste
2 cups (500 ml/16 fl oz) vegetable stock
2 tablespoons chopped fresh basil
⅔ cup (125 g/4 oz) Kalamata olives, pitted
1–2 teaspoons soft brown sugar

1 Put the beans in a large bowl, cover with cold water and soak overnight. Rinse well, then transfer to a saucepan, cover with cold water and cook for 45 minutes, or until just tender. Drain.

2 Heat the oil in a large saucepan. Cook the garlic and onion wedges over medium heat for 2–3 minutes, or until the onion is soft. Add the red and green capsicums, and cook for a further 5 minutes.

3 Stir in the tomato, tomato paste, stock and beans. Simmer, covered, for 40 minutes, or until the beans are cooked through. Stir in the basil, olives and sugar. Season with salt and pepper. Serve hot with crusty bread.

Note: 1 cup of dried haricot beans yields about 2½ cups cooked beans. You can use 2½ cups canned haricot or borlotti beans instead if you prefer.

Cook the garlic, onion wedges and capsicum in a large saucepan.

Simmer the mixture for 40 minutes, or until the beans are cooked through.

Lamb's Liver and Bacon Stew

PREPARATION TIME: 10 minutes
TOTAL COOKING TIME: 30 minutes
SERVES 6

1 lamb's liver, about 750 g (1½ lb)
   (see Note)
¼ cup (30 g/1 oz) cornflour
¼ teaspoon ground black pepper
6 rashers bacon, cut into large pieces
2 tablespoons oil
2 onions, thinly sliced
1 beef stock cube, crumbled

1 Wash the liver and cut it into thin slices, discarding any veins or discoloured spots. Pat the liver dry with paper towels. Combine the cornflour and pepper. Toss the liver slices in the seasoned cornflour, shaking off the excess.

2 Cook the bacon in a heavy-based saucepan until crisp, then drain on paper towels. Heat the oil in the pan and cook the onion gently until golden, then remove from the pan.

3 Cook the liver quickly in small batches over medium heat until well browned, then drain on paper towels. Return the liver, bacon and onion to the pan. Dissolve the stock cube in 1 cup (250 ml/8 fl oz) boiling water, then gradually add to the pan. Stir over medium heat for 10 minutes, or until the liquid boils and thickens. Serve the stew immediately.

Note: Soaking the liver in milk for 30 minutes before cooking will result in a milder taste.

Toss the liver slices in the seasoned cornflour, shaking off the excess.

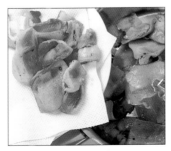

Cook the bacon in a heavy-based saucepan until crisp, then drain on paper towels.

Return the cooked bacon, liver slices and onion to the pan.

51

Beef Bourguignonne

PREPARATION TIME: 10 minutes
TOTAL COOKING TIME: 2 hours
SERVES 4

1 kg (2 lb) diced beef
1/4 cup (30 g/1 oz) seasoned plain flour
1 tablespoon oil
150 g (5 oz) bacon, diced
8 bulb spring onions, greens trimmed to 2 cm (3/4 inch)
200 g (61/2 oz) button mushrooms
2 cups (500 ml/16 fl oz) red wine
2 tablespoons tomato paste
2 cups (500 ml/16 fl oz) beef stock
1 bouquet garni (see Note)

1 Toss the beef in the seasoned flour until evenly coated, shaking off any excess. Heat the oil in a large saucepan over high heat. Cook the beef in three batches for about 3 minutes, or until well browned all over, adding a little extra oil as needed. Remove from the pan.

2 Add the bacon to the pan and cook for 2 minutes, or until browned. Remove with a slotted spoon and add to the beef. Add the spring onions and mushrooms, and cook for 5 minutes, or until the onions are browned. Remove.

3 Slowly pour the red wine into the pan, scraping up any sediment from the bottom with a wooden spoon. Stir in the tomato paste and stock. Add the bouquet garni and return the beef, bacon and any juices. Bring to the boil, then reduce the heat and simmer for 45 minutes. Return the spring onions and mushrooms to the pan. Cook for 1 hour, or until the meat is very tender and the sauce is glossy. Serve with steamed new potatoes or mash.

Note: To make a bouquet garni, wrap the green part of a leek around a bay leaf, a sprig of thyme, a sprig of parsley and celery leaves, and tie with string. The combination of herbs can be varied according to taste.

Toss the diced beef in the seasoned flour until evenly coated.

Slowly pour the red wine into the pan, scraping up any sediment with a wooden spoon.

Creamy Garlic Seafood Stew

PREPARATION TIME: 20 minutes
TOTAL COOKING TIME: 20 minutes
SERVES 6

12 scallops, with roe
500 g (1 lb) skinless firm white fish fillets
  (see Note)
6 raw Balmain bugs or crabs
500 g (1 lb) raw medium prawns
50 g (1¾ oz) butter
1 onion, finely chopped
5–6 large cloves garlic, finely chopped
½ cup (125 ml/4 fl oz) white wine
2 cups (500 ml/16 fl oz) cream
1½ tablespoons Dijon mustard
2 teaspoons lemon juice
2 tablespoons chopped fresh flat-leaf parsley

1 Slice or pull off any membrane or hard muscle from the scallops. Cut the fish into 2 cm (¾ inch) cubes. Cut the heads off the bugs, then use kitchen scissors to cut down around the sides of the tail so you can flap open the shell. Remove the flesh in one piece, then slice each piece in half. Peel and devein the prawns. Refrigerate all the seafood, covered, until ready to use.

2 Melt the butter in a frying pan and cook the onion and garlic over medium heat for 2 minutes, or until the onion is softened (be careful not to burn the garlic—it may turn bitter).

3 Add the wine to the pan and cook for 4 minutes, or until reduced by half. Stir in the cream, mustard and lemon juice, and simmer for 5–6 minutes, or until reduced to almost half.

4 Add the prawns to the pan and cook for 1 minute, then add the bug meat and cook for another minute, or until white. Add the fish and cook for 2 minutes, or until cooked through (the flesh will flake easily when tested with a fork). Finally, add the scallops and cook for 1 minute. If any of the seafood is still not cooked, cook for another minute or so, but be careful not to overcook as this will result in tough flesh. Remove the frying pan from the heat and toss the parsley through. Season to taste. Serve with salad and bread.

Note: Try using perch, ling, bream, tuna or blue-eye.

Use strong kitchen scissors to cut through the sides of each bug tail.

Pull back the shell and pull out the bug flesh in one piece.

Simmer the sauce for about 5 minutes, or until reduced to almost half.

Greek Octopus Stew

PREPARATION TIME: 25 minutes
TOTAL COOKING TIME: 1 hour 10 minutes
SERVES 4–6

1 kg (2 lb) baby octopus
2 tablespoons olive oil
1 large onion, chopped
3 cloves garlic, crushed
1 bay leaf
3 cups (750 ml/24 fl oz) red wine
1/4 cup (60 ml/2 fl oz) red wine vinegar
400 g (13 oz) can crushed tomatoes
1 tablespoon tomato paste
1 tablespoon chopped fresh oregano
1/4 teaspoon ground cinnamon
small pinch ground cloves
1 teaspoon sugar
2 tablespoons finely chopped fresh flat-leaf
    parsley

1 Cut between the head and tentacles of the octopus, just below the eyes. Grasp the body and push the beak out and up through the centre of the tentacles with your fingers. Cut the eyes from the head by slicing off a small round. Discard the eye section. Carefully slit through one side, avoiding the ink sac, and remove any gut from inside. Rinse the octopus well under running water.

2 Heat the oil in a large saucepan, add the onion and cook over medium heat for 5 minutes, or until starting to brown. Add the garlic and bay leaf, and cook for 1 minute further. Add the octopus and stir to coat in the onion mixture.

3 Stir in the wine, vinegar, tomato, tomato paste, oregano, cinnamon, cloves and sugar. Bring to the boil, then reduce the heat and simmer for 1 hour, or until the octopus is tender and the sauce has thickened slightly. Stir in the parsley and season with salt and ground black pepper. Serve with a Greek salad and crusty bread to mop up the delicious juices.

Cut between the head and the tentacles of the octopus.

Slit the head section and remove any gut from the inside.

Add the octopus to the pan and stir to coat in the onion mixture.

Steak and Kidney Stew

PREPARATION TIME: 35 minutes
TOTAL COOKING TIME: 2 hours 30 minutes
SERVES 4–6

1 kg (2 lb) chuck steak, trimmed
8 lamb's kidneys
1/4 cup (60 ml/2 fl oz) oil
1 rasher bacon, rind removed, cut into long,
  thin strips
40 g (11/4 oz) butter
1 large onion, chopped
300 g (10 oz) button mushrooms, halved
1 cup (250 ml/8 fl oz) Muscat
2–3 cloves garlic, crushed
1/4 teaspoon ground allspice
1/2 teaspoon paprika
2 teaspoons coriander seeds, lightly crushed
1 tablespoon wholegrain mustard
1 cup (250 ml/8 fl oz) beef stock
2–3 tablespoons soft brown sugar
1–2 teaspoons fresh thyme
1–2 teaspoons fresh rosemary

1 Cut the steak into 2–3 cm (1 inch) cubes. Cut the kidneys in half, remove the core and any fat, then slice them in half again.

2 Heat 1 teaspoon of the oil in a large, heavy-based saucepan. Add the bacon and cook over medium heat until just crisp. Remove and set aside.

3 Heat 2 tablespoons of the oil and 30 g (1 oz) of the butter in the pan. Brown the steak cubes in batches, then set aside.

4 Add the onion to the pan and cook for 3 minutes, or until soft and golden. Add the mushrooms and cook, stirring, for 3 minutes, until starting to brown. Stir in half the Muscat and simmer for 3–4 minutes. Remove and set aside.

5 Add the remaining oil and butter to the pan. Stir in the garlic, allspice, paprika and coriander, and cook for 1 minute. Add the kidney and cook until just starting to brown. Stir in the mustard and remaining Muscat, and simmer for 2 minutes.

6 Stir in the bacon, steak, onion and mushrooms. Stir in the stock, bring to the boil, then reduce the heat, cover and simmer for 1 hour. Add the sugar. Simmer, covered, for 40 minutes, then uncovered for 20 minutes, stirring in the herbs during the last 10 minutes.

Halve the kidneys and remove the cores and fat. Slice in half again.

Add half the Muscat to the onion and mushrooms, and simmer for 3–4 minutes.

Add the kidney to the pan-fried spices and cook until just starting to brown.

Pork and Eggplant Hotpot

PREPARATION TIME: 20 minutes
TOTAL COOKING TIME: 1 hour 40 minutes
SERVES 4

olive oil, for cooking
375 g (12 oz) slender eggplant, cut into
   3 cm (1¼ inch) slices
8 bulb spring onions
400 g (13 oz) can chopped tomatoes
2 cloves garlic, crushed
2 teaspoons ground cumin
500 g (1 lb) pork fillet, cut into 3 cm
   (1¼ inch) thick slices
seasoned plain flour
2/3 cup (170 ml/5½ fl oz) cider
1 sprig fresh rosemary
2 tablespoons finely chopped toasted
   almonds

1 Heat ¼ cup (60 ml/2 fl oz) of oil in a large, heavy-based frying pan. Brown the eggplant in batches over high heat, adding oil as needed. Remove and set aside.

2 Quarter the spring onions along their length. Add some oil to the pan and fry the spring onion over medium heat for 5 minutes. Add the tomato, garlic and cumin, and cook for 2 minutes. Remove and set aside.

3 Coat the pork in the seasoned flour, shaking off any excess. Brown in batches over medium–high heat until golden, adding oil as needed. Remove and set aside.

4 Add the cider to the pan and stir well, scraping down the side and base. Allow to boil for 1–2 minutes, then add ½ cup (125 ml/4 fl oz) water. Reduce the heat and stir in the spring onion and tomato. Add the pork, season, and poke the rosemary sprig into the stew. Partially cover and simmer gently for 20 minutes.

5 Layer the eggplant on top, partially cover and cook for 25 minutes, or until the pork is tender. Just before serving, gently toss the almonds through.

Fry the eggplant in batches over high heat until browned on both sides.

Add the cider to the frying pan, scraping the brown bits from the side and base.

Layer the eggplant over the top of the pork and tomato mixture.

Moroccan Seafood with Coriander

PREPARATION TIME: 50 minutes
TOTAL COOKING TIME: 50 minutes
SERVES 6

2 tablespoons olive oil
2 red onions, roughly chopped
1 red capsicum, chopped
4 cloves garlic, crushed
2 teaspoons ground cumin
1 teaspoon ground coriander
2 teaspoons sweet paprika
1/2 teaspoon dried chilli flakes
1 cup (250 ml/8 fl oz) chicken or fish stock
425 g (14 oz) can chopped tomatoes
1/3 cup (80 ml/2³/4 fl oz) orange juice
1 tablespoon sugar
1/4 cup (40 g/1¹/4 oz) seedless raisins
375 g (12 oz) baby new potatoes
500 g (1 lb) baby octopus, cleaned
12 raw king prawns, peeled and deveined,
   tails intact
1 kg (2 lb) thick white fish fillets, cut into
   chunks

Coriander Puree
1 cup (30 g/1 oz) fresh coriander
   leaves
2 tablespoons ground almonds
1/3 cup (80 ml/2³/4 fl oz) extra virgin
   olive oil
1/2 teaspoon ground cumin
1 teaspoon honey

1 Heat the olive oil in a large saucepan and cook the onion over medium heat for about 5 minutes, or until soft. Add the capsicum and garlic, and cook for another minute. Add the cumin, coriander, paprika and chilli flakes, and cook until fragrant.

2 Pour in the stock, tomato, orange juice, sugar and raisins, and bring to the boil. Add the potatoes, reduce the heat to low and gently simmer for 20–30 minutes, or until the potatoes are just tender. Season to taste.

3 Use a small sharp knife to remove the octopus heads; slit the heads open and remove the gut. Grasp the body firmly and push the beak out with your index finger; remove and discard. Add the octopus, prawns and fish to the pan and cook, covered, for 10 minutes, or until the fish flakes when tested with a fork.

4 To make the coriander purée, place the coriander leaves and ground almonds in a food processor. With the motor running, drizzle in the oil and process until smooth, then add the cumin, honey and salt to taste. Process until well combined.

5 To serve, dish the stew onto serving plates and drizzle a spoonful of purée on top. Serve with couscous and a green leaf salad.

Peel and devein the prawns, and cut the cleaned octopus into bite-sized pieces.

Process the coriander leaves and ground almonds, gradually drizzling in the oil.

63

Vegetarian Chilli

PREPARATION TIME: 15 minutes +
10 minutes soaking
TOTAL COOKING TIME: 40 minutes
SERVES 6–8

3/4 cup (130 g/4¹/₂ oz) burghul (cracked
   wheat)
2 tablespoons olive oil
1 large onion, finely chopped
2 cloves garlic, crushed
1 teaspoon chilli powder
2 teaspoons ground cumin
1 teaspoon cayenne pepper
¹/₂ teaspoon ground cinnamon
2 x 400 g (13 oz) cans crushed tomatoes
3 cups (750 ml/24 fl oz) vegetable stock
440 g (14 oz) can red kidney beans, rinsed
   and drained
2 x 300 g (10 oz) cans chickpeas, rinsed and
   drained
310 g (10 oz) can corn kernels, drained
2 tablespoons tomato paste
corn chips and sour cream

1 Soak the burghul with 1 cup (250 ml/8 fl oz) hot water for 10 minutes. Heat the oil in a large heavy-based saucepan and cook the onion for 10 minutes, stirring often, until soft and golden.
2 Add the garlic, chilli powder, cumin, cayenne and cinnamon, and cook, stirring, for 1 minute.
3 Add the tomato, stock and burghul. Bring to the boil and simmer for 10 minutes. Stir in the beans, drained chickpeas, corn and tomato paste, and simmer for 20 minutes, stirring often. Serve with corn chips and sour cream.

Stir the garlic and spices into the pan with the onion, and cook for 1 minute.

Add the crushed tomato, stock and burghul to the pan.

Stir in the beans, chickpeas, corn kernels and tomato paste.

65

Chilli Con Pollo

PREPARATION TIME: 10 minutes
TOTAL COOKING TIME: 45 minutes
SERVES 4

1 tablespoon olive oil
1 onion, finely chopped
500 g (1 lb) chicken mince
1–2 teaspoons mild chilli powder
440 g (14 oz) can chopped tomatoes
2 tablespoons tomato paste
1–2 teaspoons soft brown sugar
425 g (14 oz) can red kidney beans, rinsed
  and drained

1 Heat the oil in a large saucepan. Add the chopped onion and cook over medium heat for 3 minutes, or until soft. Increase the heat to high and add the chicken mince. Cook until the chicken has browned, breaking up any lumps with a wooden spoon.

2 Add the chilli powder to the chicken and cook for 1 minute. Stir in the tomato, tomato paste and ½ cup (125 ml/4 fl oz) water.

3 Bring to the boil, then reduce the heat and simmer for 30 minutes. Stir through the sugar to taste and the kidney beans. Season. Serve with corn chips or in taco shells with sour cream.

Add the chicken mince to the onion and cook until browned, breaking up any lumps.

Stir the tomato, tomato paste and water into the chicken mixture.

After 30 minutes, stir in the sugar and drained kidney beans.

67

Spanish Chicken and Rice Stew

PREPARATION TIME: 10 minutes
TOTAL COOKING TIME: 1 hour
SERVES 4

1/4 cup (60 ml/2 fl oz) olive oil
4 chicken thighs and 6 drumsticks
1 large red onion, finely chopped
1 large green capsicum, two-thirds diced
  and one-third julienned
3 teaspoons sweet paprika
400 g (13 oz) can diced tomatoes
1 1/4 cups (275 g/9 oz) paella or arborio rice
  (see Note)
1/2 teaspoon ground saffron

1 Heat 2 tablespoons of the oil in a large deep frying pan over high heat. Season the chicken pieces well and brown in batches. Remove the chicken from the pan.

2 Reduce the heat to medium and add the remaining oil. Add the onion and the diced capsicum, and cook gently for 5 minutes. Stir in the sweet paprika and cook for 30 seconds. Add the tomato and simmer for 1–3 minutes, or until it thickens.

3 Stir in 3½ cups (875 ml/28 fl oz) boiling water, then add the rice and saffron. Return the chicken to the pan and stir to combine. Season to taste. Bring to the boil, then cover, reduce the heat to medium–low and simmer for 20–30 minutes, or until the liquid has been absorbed and the chicken is tender. Stir in the julienned capsicum, then allow to stand, covered, for 3–4 minutes before serving.

Note: Paella rice is a medium round grain from Spain. Calasparra is the most commonly available variety and can be purchased from fine food stores or Spanish delicatessens.

Add the tomato to the capsicum mixture, and simmer until it thickens.

Simmer until the liquid has been absorbed and the chicken is tender.

Ratatouille

PREPARATION TIME: 30 minutes
TOTAL COOKING TIME: 40 minutes
SERVES 4–6

100 ml (3¹/₂ fl oz) olive oil
500 g (1 lb) eggplant, cut into 2 cm (³/₄ inch) cubes
375 g (12 oz) zucchini, cut into 2 cm (³/₄ inch) slices
1 green capsicum, seeded, cut into 2 cm (³/₄ inch) cubes
1 red onion, cut into 2 cm (³/₄ inch) wedges
3 cloves garlic, finely chopped
¹/₄ teaspoon cayenne pepper
2 teaspoons chopped fresh thyme
2 bay leaves
6 vine-ripened tomatoes, peeled and roughly chopped
1 tablespoon red wine vinegar
1 teaspoon caster sugar
¹/₄ cup (15 g/¹/₂ oz) shredded fresh basil

1 Heat 2 tablespoons of the oil in a large saucepan and cook the eggplant over medium heat for 4–5 minutes, or until soft but not browned. Remove all the eggplant from the pan.

2 Add 2 tablespoons oil to the pan and cook the zucchini slices for 3–4 minutes, or until softened. Remove the zucchini from the pan. Add the capsicum to the pan, cook for 2 minutes, then remove.

3 Heat the remaining oil in the pan, add the onion wedges and cook for 2–3 minutes, or until softened. Add the garlic, cayenne pepper, thyme and bay leaves, and cook, stirring, for 1 minute. Return the cooked eggplant, zucchini and capsicum to the pan, and add the tomato, vinegar and sugar. Simmer for 20 minutes, stirring occasionally. Stir in the basil and season with salt and black pepper. Serve hot or cold.

Note: Ratatouille takes quite a long time to prepare and so is traditionally made in large quantities. It is then eaten over several days as an hors d'oeuvre, side dish or main meal.

Peel the skin away from the crosses cut in the base of the tomatoes.

Cook the eggplant until softened but not browned, then remove.

Cook the eggplant until softened but not browned, then remove.

Stuffed Squid Stew

PREPARATION TIME: 50 minutes
TOTAL COOKING TIME: 50 minutes
SERVES 4

100 ml (3½ fl oz) olive oil
1 large onion, finely chopped
2 cloves garlic, crushed
1 cup (80 g/2¾ oz) fresh breadcrumbs
1 egg, lightly beaten
60 g (2 oz) kefalotyri cheese, grated
60 g (2 oz) haloumi cheese, grated
4 large or 8 small squid (1 kg/2 lb), cleaned
  (see Note)
1 small onion, finely chopped, extra
2 cloves garlic, crushed, extra
500 g (1 lb) firm ripe tomatoes, peeled and
  diced
150 ml (5 fl oz) red wine
1 tablespoon chopped fresh oregano
1 tablespoon chopped fresh flat-leaf parsley

1 Heat 2 tablespoons of the oil in a frying pan, add the onion and cook over medium heat for 3 minutes. Remove. Combine with the garlic, breadcrumbs, egg and cheese. Season.

2 Pat the squid hoods dry with paper towels and, using a teaspoon, fill them three-quarters full with the stuffing. Do not pack them too tightly or the stuffing mixture will swell and burst out during cooking. Secure the ends with wooden toothpicks.

3 Heat the remaining oil in a large frying pan, add the squid and cook for 1–2 minutes on all sides. Remove. Add the extra onion and cook over medium heat for 3 minutes, or until soft, then add the extra garlic and cook for a further 1 minute. Stir in the tomato and wine, and simmer for 10 minutes, or until thick and pulpy, then stir in the oregano and parsley. Return the squid to the pan and cook, covered, for 20–25 minutes, or until tender. Serve warm with the tomato sauce or cool with a salad.

Note: Ask the fishmonger to clean the squid. Or, discard the tentacles and cartilage. Rinse the hoods under running water and pull off the skin.

Fill the squid hoods three-quarters full with the stuffing mixture.

Cook the stuffed squid hoods in a frying pan on all sides.

Add the squid to the tomato mixture and cook until tender.

Creamy Veal and Mushroom Stew

PREPARATION TIME: 20 minutes

TOTAL COOKING TIME: 2 hours

SERVES 4

750 g (1½ lb) veal steaks, cut into 1 cm (½ inch) strips
¼ cup (30 g/1 oz) plain flour
30 g (1 oz) butter
1 clove garlic, crushed
1 tablespoon Dijon mustard
1 cup (250 ml/8 fl oz) cream
½ cup (125 ml/4 fl oz) white wine
1 tablespoon chopped fresh thyme
1 cup (250 ml/8 fl oz) chicken stock
375 g (12 oz) button mushrooms, halved

1 Toss the meat in the flour, shaking off the excess. Heat the butter and garlic in a heavy-based saucepan. Add the meat and cook quickly in small batches over medium heat until well browned. Drain on paper towels.

2 Return the meat to the pan and add the mustard, cream, wine, thyme and stock. Bring to the boil, then reduce the heat and simmer, covered, for 1½ hours, stirring occasionally.

3 Add the mushrooms and cook for a further 15 minutes, or until the meat is tender. Delicious served with pasta and steamed vegetables.

Toss the veal strips in the flour, shaking off any excess flour.

Return the meat to the pan with the mustard, cream, wine, thyme and stock.

Add the mushrooms and cook for a further 15 minutes, or until the meat is tender.

75

Lemon and Rosemary Chicken Stew

PREPARATION TIME: 10 minutes
TOTAL COOKING TIME: 30 minutes
SERVES 4

8 large chicken drumsticks
60 g (2 oz) butter
2 cloves garlic, crushed
2 teaspoons finely grated lemon rind
2 tablespoons chopped fresh rosemary
1 tablespoon plain flour
1½ cups (375 ml/12 fl oz) chicken stock
2 tablespoons lemon juice

1 Using a sharp knife, make two deep cuts in the thickest part of each chicken drumstick.
2 Melt the butter in a large frying pan. Add the drumsticks and cook over medium heat for 2 minutes on each side, or until brown. Add the garlic, lemon rind and rosemary.
3 Blend the flour, stock and lemon juice until smooth. Add to the pan and bring to the boil. Reduce the heat and simmer, covered, for 25 minutes, or until the drumsticks are tender, stirring occasionally. Season, and serve immediately.

HINT: To check whether chicken is cooked, insert a skewer into the thickest part. If the juice runs clear, the chicken is cooked.

Make two deep cuts in the thickest part of the chicken drumsticks.

Add the crushed garlic, lemon rind and rosemary to the drumsticks.

Pour the stock mixture into the pan, then bring to the boil.

Beef Pot Roast

PREPARATION TIME: 15 minutes
TOTAL COOKING TIME: 3 hours 15 minutes
SERVES 6

300 g (10 oz) baby brown onions
2 carrots
3 parsnips, peeled
40 g (1¼ oz) butter
1–1.5 kg (2–3 lb) eye of silverside, trimmed
   of fat (see Note)
¼ cup (60 ml/2 fl oz) dry red wine
1 large tomato, finely chopped
1 cup (250 ml/8 fl oz) beef stock
mild or hot English mustard, to serve

1 Put the onions in a heatproof bowl
and cover with boiling water. Leave
for 1 minute, then drain well. Allow
to cool, then peel off the skins.
2 Cut the carrots and parsnips in half
lengthways, then into even-sized
pieces. Heat half the butter in a
large heavy-based saucepan that
will tightly fit the meat (it will shrink
during cooking), add the onions,

carrot and parsnip, and cook, stirring, over
medium–high heat until browned. Remove from
the pan. Add the remaining butter to the pan and
add the meat, browning well all over. Increase the
heat to high and pour in the wine. Bring to the
boil, then add the tomato and stock. Return to
the boil, then reduce the heat to low, cover and
simmer for 2 hours, turning once. Add the
vegetables and simmer, covered, for 1 hour.
3 Remove the meat from the pan and put it on a
board ready for carving. Cover with foil and leave
it to stand while finishing the sauce.
4 Increase the heat to high and boil the pan juices
with the vegetables for 10 minutes to reduce and
thicken slightly. Skim off any excess fat, and taste
before seasoning. Slice the meat and arrange on a
serving platter or individual serving plates with the
vegetables. Drizzle generously with the pan juices.
Serve with mustard.

Note: Eye of silverside is a tender, long-shaped cut
of silverside that carves easily into serving-sized
pieces. A regular piece of silverside or topside may
be substituted.

Put the baby brown onions in a
bowl and cover with boiling
water.

Add the butter and meat to the
pan, and brown the meat well
on all sides.

Add the vegetables to the meat,
then cover and simmer for 1
hour.

All our recipes are thoroughly tested in a specially developed test kitchen. Standard metric measuring cups and spoons are used in the development of our recipes. All cup and spoon measurements are level. We have used 60 g (2¼ oz/Grade 3) eggs in all recipes. Sizes of cans vary from manufacturer to manufacturer and between countries – use the can size closest to the one suggested in the recipe.

CONVERSION GUIDE

1 cup = 250 ml (9 fl oz)

1 teaspoon = 5 ml

1 Australian tablespoon = 20 ml (4 teaspoons)

1 UK/US tablespoon = 15 ml (3 teaspoons)

Where temperature ranges are indicated, the lower figure applies to gas ovens, the higher to electric ovens. This allows for the fact that the flame in gas ovens generates a drier heat, which effectively cooks food faster than the moister heat of an electric oven, even if the temperature setting is the same.

DRY MEASURES	LIQUID MEASURES	LINEAR MEASURES
30 g = 1 oz	30 ml = 1 fl oz	6 mm = ¼ inch
250 g = 9 oz	125 ml = 4 fl oz	1 cm = ½ inch
500 g = 1 lb 2 oz	250 ml = 9 fl oz	2.5 cm = 1 inch

	°C	°F	GAS MARK
Very slow	120	250	½
Slow	150	300	2
Mod slow	160	325	3
Moderate	180	350	4
Mod hot	190(g)–210(e)	375–425	5
Hot	200(g)–240(e)	400–475	6
Very hot	230(g)–260(e)	450–525	8

CUP CONVERSIONS – DRY INGREDIENTS

1 cup almonds, slivered whole = 125 g (4½ oz)

1 cup cheese, lightly packed processed cheddar = 155 g (5½oz)

1 cup wheat flour = 125 g (4½ oz)

1 cup wholemeal flour = 140 g (5 oz)

1 cup minced (ground) meat = 250 g (9 oz)

1 cup pasta shapes = 125 g (4½ oz)

1 cup raisins = 170 g (6 oz)

1 cup rice, short grain, raw = 200 g (7 oz)

1 cup sesame seeds = 160 g (6 oz)

1 cup split peas = 250 g (9 oz)

(g) = gas (e) = electric

Note: For fan-forced ovens, check your appliance manual, but as a general rule, set the oven temperature to 20°C lower than the temperature indicated in the recipe.

INTERNATIONAL GLOSSARY

capsicum	sweet bell pepper	cornflour	cornstarch
chick pea	garbanzo bean	eggplant	aubergine
chilli	chile, chili pepper	spring onion	scallion
		zucchini	courgette

Murdoch Books Pty Limited

Erico House, 6th Floor North, 93-99 Upper Richmond Road, Putney, London, SW15 2TG, United Kingdom.

This edition published in 2007 for Index Books Ltd, Garrard Way, Kettering, NN16 8TD, United Kingdom.

ISBN-13: 978 1 921259 72 2   ISBN-10: 1 921259 72 8

Printed by Sing Cheong Printing Co. Ltd. PRINTED IN CHINA.